MAKE it WORK!

SPACE

Andrew Haslam

written by
David Glover

Photography
Jon Barnes

PRINCETON ■ LONDON

MAKE it WORK!
Titles in the series

Body
Building
Dinosaurs
Earth
Electricity
Flight
Insects
Machines
Photography
Plants
Ships
Sound
Space
Time

Published in the United States and Canada by
Two-Can Publishing LLC, 234 Nassau Street, Princeton NJ 08542

© 1998 Two-Can Publishing
This edition © 2000 Two-Can Publishing LLC
Design © 1998 Andrew Haslam and Wendy Baker

**For information on other Two-Can books and multimedia,
call 1-609-921-6700, fax 1-609-921-3349, or visit our Web site at
http://www.two-canpublishing.com**

Library of Congress Cataloging-in-Publication Data
Haslam, Andrew.
    Space / Andrew Haslam; written by David Glover; photography by Jon Barnes.
        p. cm. — (Make it work!)
        Summary: An illustrated book of projects that demonstrate how the universe works.
    ISBN 1-58728-366-2 (hc) — ISBN 1-58728-362-X (sc)
    1. Astronomy—Experiments—Juvenile literature.
    2. Astronomy—Study and teaching—Activity programs—Juvenile literature.
    [1. Astronomy—Experiments. 2. Experiments. 3. Universe]
    I. Glover, David, 1953 Sept. 4- II. Barnes, John, ill. III. Title. IV. Series.
    QB46.H23 1998
    520'.78—dc21   98-13401

Printed in Hong Kong
(hc) 1 2 3 4 5 6 7 8 9 10 02 01 00
(sc) 1 2 3 4 5 6 7 8 9 10 02 01 00

Series Editor: Kate Asser
Editor: Christine Morley
Assistant editors: Jacqueline McCann, Robert Sved
Series concept and design: Andrew Haslam and Wendy Baker
Additional design: Paul Miller

**NOTE: Insulated wire should be used for all projects in which batteries and wire
are required.**

Contents

Words marked in **bold** in the
text are explained in the glossary.

You can do many exciting things as an astronomer: study the sun and moon, plan rocket expeditions to explore the planets, search for **black holes**, and come up with theories about how the universe began and how it might end.

MAKE it WORK!

You don't need expensive or complicated equipment to be an astronomer. With just a warm coat and a star chart, you can go outside on a clear night and start to learn the names of the stars. Building the models in this book will show you the differences between the planets, stars, and **galaxies** that you spot and help you to understand how the universe works.

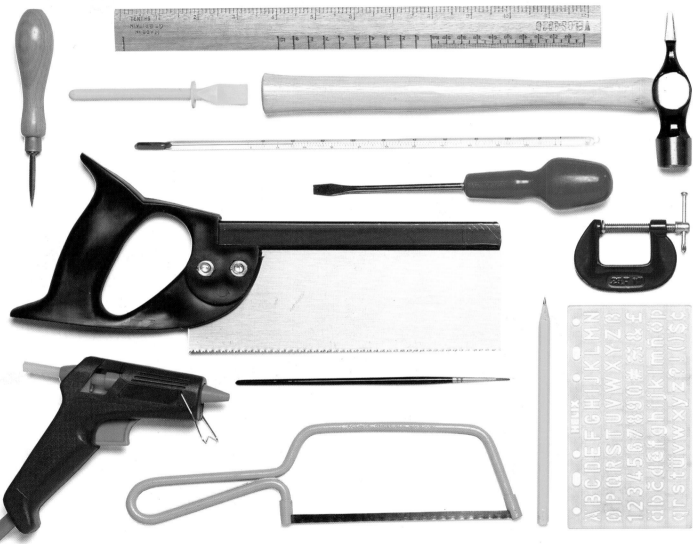

Now is a very exciting time in the history of astronomy. Powerful telescopes, modern computers, and sophisticated **space probes** help astronomers to see farther and more clearly into space than ever before.

You will need

You can build most of the models out of cheap, easily available materials, such as cardboard, wood, marbles, plastic containers, and other odds and ends. You will need some tools to cut the materials; all of the equipment above will be very useful as part of your astronomer's kit.

Using lights

Some of the projects use light bulbs powered by batteries. Flashlights are also used, and the bulbs in these and the battery-operated bulbs are safe to handle. However, if you use a low-voltage lamp, always ask an adult to set it up for you.

Warning! Never look at the sun through binoculars or a telescope.

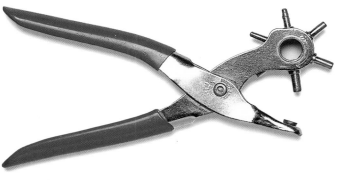

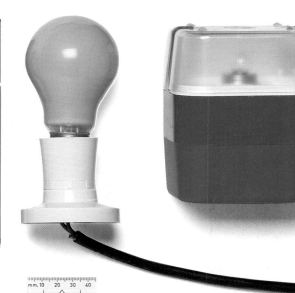

You will need some simple tools to plan projects and to record observations. Star charts, which you can find in astronomy books or buy separately, are a handy way to find your way around the night sky. Binoculars, **lenses**, and a **magnetic compass** will all be useful.

Safety!

Sharp tools are dangerous! Take care when you use them and ask an adult to help you. Make sure that anything you are cutting or drilling is held firmly so that it cannot slip. A small table vise is ideal for holding pieces of wood.

6 Day and Night

Ancient peoples believed that Earth was the center of the universe. Their belief was based on what they could feel and see—Earth under our feet feels as if it is still, and it looks as though the sun, the moon, and the stars move around Earth. But now we know that it is really Earth that moves around the sun. The sun only appears to be moving through the sky because Earth spins on its **axis** as it travels through space.

MAKE it WORK!

This model of the sun, Earth, and moon shows how Earth's spin gives us day and night.

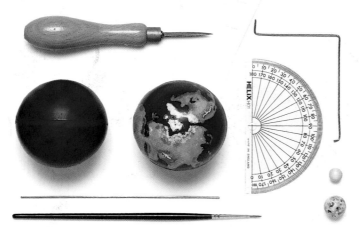

You will need
tape
modeling clay
an awl
a protractor
a small rubber ball
two pieces of wire
a paintbrush and paints
a large sponge rubber ball
a light bulb in a holder or
   a bright flashlight
a wooden or plastic bead

1 The large sponge rubber ball is Earth. Paint a map of the world on it, using green, yellow, and blue paint. Use white to show the ice at the poles.

2 Ask an adult to help you make a hole through Earth, from pole to pole, with the awl.

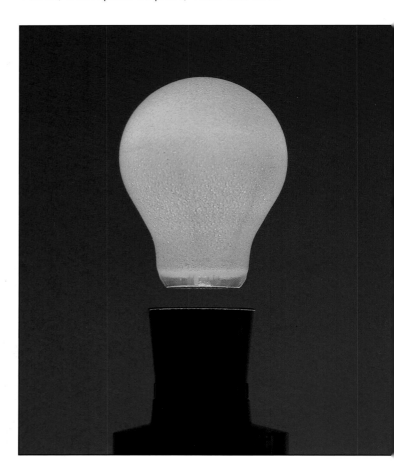

3 Push Earth onto one piece of wire and slip the bead onto the foot of the wire. Fix the wire to a flat base with some modeling clay.

4 The light bulb is the sun. Earth **orbits** the sun, spinning on its axis (the wire in the model) as it moves. The axis is tilted to the orbit by 23°. Show this in your model by fixing the wire to the protractor at 67° from the horizontal.

5 Add the small ball to your model by fixing it on a bent wire, as shown. This is the moon. Push the wire into the hole in the bead. The moon orbits Earth.

The sun is our nearest star. It is a huge ball of flame, 93 million miles away, that warms Earth. The sun's power comes from a **nuclear reaction** called fusion. Without the warmth of the sun, Earth would be a cold, lifeless ball of rock.

Earth is a planet in orbit around the sun. It is about 8,000 miles in diameter and is the only planet in the solar system with liquid water on its surface. At the North and South poles, which get very little sunlight, the water has frozen into ice caps.

  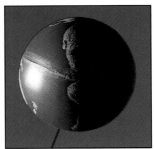 

On the side of Earth facing the sun it is daytime. The side facing away from the sun is in the dark shadow of night. Earth spins on its axis, completing a rotation once every 24 hours. Try turning your Earth model to see how different places on Earth move from day to night.

Looking down on the North Pole, Earth spins counterclockwise. This means that we are moving from west to east. As we move from the night shadow into daylight, the sun seems to rise in the east. At the end of the day, the sun appears to set in the west.

We use the motion of Earth to measure time. It takes a day (24 hours) for Earth to spin once on its axis and 365¼ days for Earth to orbit the sun. Shadows cast by objects blocking the sun's light move as Earth spins. You can chart the shadows throughout the day with a sundial and use it to tell the time.

You will need

glue	tape
scissors	a watch
a craft knife	a stencil
cardboard, poster board	a rubber band
a small magnetic compass with a moving scale	

1 For the sundial base, cut two rectangles of thick cardboard, 6 in. x 3 in. Then cut out two rectangles of poster board to the same dimensions and glue them on top of the cardboard. Join the rectangles together on one side only with tape.

gnomon

MAKE it WORK!

Sundials were probably the first clocks. You can make a simple sundial by sticking a pole in the ground and marking the position of its shadow with stones at different times of the day. The portable sundial, above, has a compass, so that you can line it up with north each time you use it.

2 Cut out a third rectangle of the poster board, 12 in. x 3 in. Ask an adult to help you cut a slit in the center. Glue this poster board to the base rectangle.

3 Cut a sundial face and three legs, one of which includes dial pointer, or **gnomon**, from poster board, as shown left. The gnomon is 3 in. long.

4 Ask an adult to help you cut a slot in the dial face for the gnomon. Fold and glue the leg flaps to assemble the sundial, as shown below. Glue the gnomon foot into the central slit.

5 Glue the compass to one end of the base. With an adult's help, cut a hole in the other end, so that the compass will rest in it when folded. Keep the sundial closed with a rubber band.

7 Now you must find north on the sundial. If you live in the Northern **Hemisphere** (for example, in the United States or Europe), then you must line up the sundial so that the straight edge of the pointer faces south. But if you live in the Southern Hemisphere (for example, in Australia or New Zealand), then the pointer should face north.

8 Look at the compass and mark north on the sundial base, as shown. If you are in the Northern Hemisphere, turn the sundial until the compass points south. If you are in the Southern Hemisphere, point the compass north. Look at your watch and, without moving the dial, mark the position of the gnomon's shadow every hour.

Calibrating your sundial

6 Now that your sundial is complete, you are ready to **calibrate** it. This means making marks to scale, at certain points on the dial, so that you can read the time from it. You will need to do this on a sunny day. Stand your sundial on a flat surface in the sun so that you can see a shadow cast by the gnomon on the face of the dial.

9 Slide off the face of the dial and number the marks, using a stencil. Carefully slide the face back into position.

When you have calibrated your sundial, you can tell the time just by lining up the compass and looking at the position of the shadow. Now you will need to use your watch only at night!

If you live north of the **equator**, the month of December falls in the middle of winter. But if you live south of the equator, it is in the middle of summer.

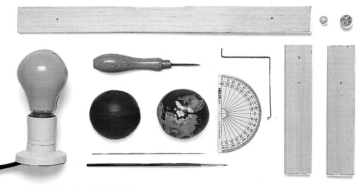

MAKE it WORK!

Building this model will help you see why the seasons—spring, summer, autumn, and winter—happen at different times north and south of the equator.

You will need

a protractor	glue
a large bead	wires
a hand drill and saw	screws
a light bulb in a holder	an awl
paint and paintbrush	a plank of wood
a small white ball	a large blue rubber ball

1 Paint a map of the world on the blue ball. With an adult's help, make a hole from pole to pole with an awl. Insert the straight wire.

2 Ask an adult to saw the wood into three strips. Glue them together to make a cross shape. Each arm represents one of the seasons.

3 Screw the light bulb (the sun) to the center of the cross.

4 Make a hole in the white ball (the moon) and mount it on bent wire, as shown below.

5 With an adult's help, drill a hole in each arm of the base for Earth's wire. Each hole must tilt by 23° to show how Earth's axis tilts. Use a protractor to guide the angle at which you drill. All four holes should tilt in the same direction.

6 Push the earth and moon wires into the bead and secure with glue. (See page 6-7)

Now you can see how the seasons occur. Below right, the Northern Hemisphere is in winter, tilted away from the sun; on the left, it is tilted toward the sun and is in summer.

In December, because of Earth's tilt, the Southern Hemisphere gets more concentrated light and heat from the sun. It is summer in the south and winter in the north.

In March and September, both hemispheres receive the same amount of light. In the north, it is spring in March and autumn in September. In the south, the seasons are reversed.

On two days each year, around March 21 and September 23, there are 12 hours of daylight and 12 hours of darkness everywhere on Earth (except at the poles). These days are called the spring and autumn equinoxes. Using your model, can you explain why the equinoxes happen on these dates?

In June, Earth is halfway around its orbit—the Northern Hemisphere is tilted toward the sun and the Southern is tilted away. So it is summer in the north and winter in the south.

In December, the sun never rises in the Arctic Circle around the North Pole, and it is dark all day. But at the South Pole, the sun never sets, and it is light at midnight. Can you see why? How long are the days at the poles in June?

The equator is never tilted far from the direct rays of the sun. This is why the seasons hardly vary in countries lying along the equator. Days and nights are always about 12 hours long.

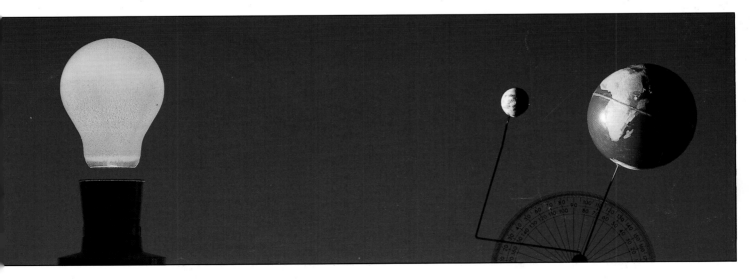

On a sunny day you can feel the heat coming off the ground, once the **energy** of the sun has heated it. The sun supplies enough energy to each square yard of Earth's surface to power several electric light bulbs. If we could trap just a fraction of this energy, we would no longer need to burn polluting fuels, such as coal and oil.

You will need

tape, cardboard, scissors
wooden dowels
two thermometers
a clay flowerpot

a large aluminum
foil pie pan
an awl, black paint
ping-pong balls

1 Make a hole in the center of the pie pan with the point of the scissors. Make a straight cut from the edge of the pan to the hole.

2 Overlap the cut edges so that the base of the pan curves like a satellite dish.

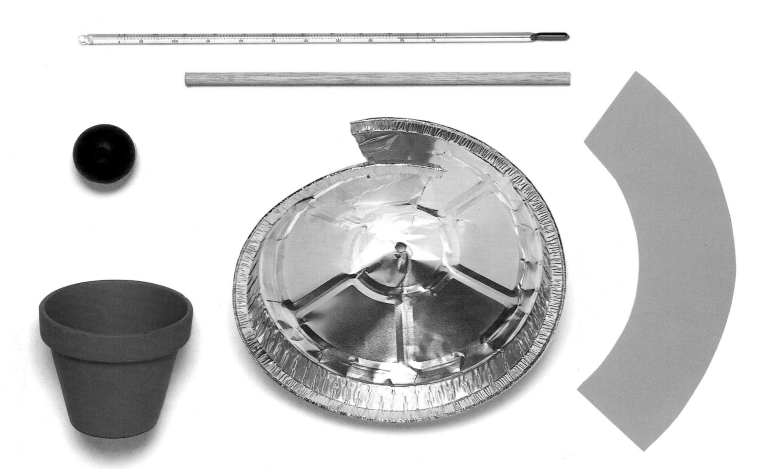

MAKE it WORK!

This simple **solar** heater uses a curved reflector to concentrate sunlight and heat the air inside a ball. Solar power stations in the United States and elsewhere use the same method. Large mirrors focus sunlight on water pipes or boilers. Steam from the boilers turns turbines to make electricity.

3 Paint a ball black. Ask an adult to use the awl to make two holes in it at 90° to each other. One hole is to mount the ball on the dowel, the other is to insert a thermometer.

4 Use cardboard and tape to fix the dish reflector at an angle on top of the flowerpot.

5 Push the dowel through the hole in the center of the pan. Mount the ball on top of the dowel. Place your solar heater in the sun. You may need to adjust the angle of the pan and the height of the ball until sunlight is reflected onto the ball.

*One solar power plant in Wisconsin has almost 10,000 reflectors. Each **solar panel** measures 3 ft. x 6 ft., and together they produce enough energy to run a large factory.*

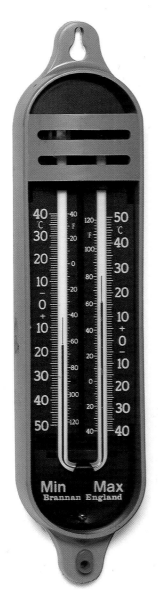

Now you are ready to test your solar heater. Use the thermometers to measure the temperature of the surrounding air and the temperature inside the ball. Because Earth is constantly spinning, you will need to move the reflector dish to keep the sun focused on the ball. In real solar power stations, the mirrors are moved automatically by computer so that they track the sun as it crosses the sky.

Black surfaces heat up more rapidly in the sun than white or silver ones. The silver surface of the pan reflects the light. The black surface of the ball absorbs the sun's energy. Make a note of the highest temperature inside the black ball. Then replace the black ball with a white ping-pong ball and repeat the experiment. Does the white ball get as hot?

14 The Moon

Earth's nearest neighbor, the moon, is a barren, uninhabitable rock that orbits Earth. The moon can be dazzling, but it does not produce light itself. We can see the moon because, like a mirror, it reflects light from the sun. The side of the moon facing the sun is brightly lit, but the side facing away from it is in dark shadow. The moon's appearance goes through a series of phases as it moves around Earth.

Use this simple model to see why the moon appears to change as it moves in its orbit.

You will need

an awl, wire	a flashlight
paint, cardboard	a blue rubber ball

1 Paint the ball black, gray, and white to make a model moon, as below.

2 Ask an adult to help make a hole through the moon with an awl and mount it on the wire.

3 Fix the flashlight at eye level and darken the rest of the room. The flashlight is the sun.

New Moon

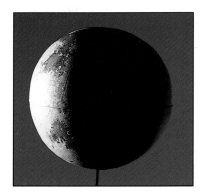

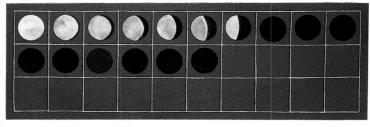

MAKE it WORK!

The moon takes 27½ days to orbit Earth. As the moon travels around Earth, we see different parts of its sunlit face. When the side of the moon facing us has no sunlight on it, we can't see it. This is the new moon. The moon's phases repeat every 29½ days.

4 Hold the moon by the wire, face the flashlight, and position the moon between your head (Earth) and the flashlight (the sun). You can see only the side of the moon in shadow. This is a new moon, as above left.

5 Now move the moon in a counterclockwise orbit. At first you see a bright crescent, then a half-lit moon. When the moon is halfway around its orbit you can look directly toward the brightly lit side. This is a full moon. As the moon continues its path, the changes reverse. Paint the moon's phases on a 30-day chart on cardboard.

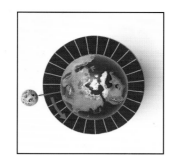

At times the moon appears brightly lit, and at other times it is shaded. But whatever its phase, the moon always shows the same face to Earth. The model above shows how the moon turns as it orbits, keeping one side hidden from view. The dark side of the moon has been seen only by the Apollo astronauts.

2 Push Earth onto the straight wire and slip the bead onto the foot of the wire. Pass this wire through the center of the dish and secure it to a base with some clay. Add the moon by fixing it onto the bent wire and threading the other end of the bent wire into the bead. (See page 6-7)

Full Moon

You will need
paint, cardboard, wire
a rubber ball (Earth)
a small ball (the moon)

modeling clay, a bead
an awl
a protractor

3 The moon orbits counterclockwise around Earth's equator. Mark the direction in which the moon travels with an arrow.

As you turn the moon around Earth, it turns with the wire, always showing the same face to Earth.

*The moon is 250,000 mi. from Earth and has a diameter of 2,160 mi., which means that it is approximately a quarter of the size of Earth. Because the phases of the moon repeat every 29 1/2 days, we divide our years into 12 months. There is not an exact number of days in a **lunar** month, nor an exact number of lunar months in a year, so we have created months with 28, 29, 30, and 31 days. The full moon occurs at a different time each month.*

1 Paint the model Earth and moon. Now cut a disk of cardboard and, using a protractor, mark every 13.3° on the disk to show the moon's motion each day. You should have 27 lines.

On July 20, 1969, Neil Armstrong became the first person to set foot on the moon. He traveled from Earth with Edwin Aldrin and Michael Collins. The astronauts were launched into space inside a capsule on top of Saturn V, one of the most powerful rockets ever built. Their mission was called Apollo 11.

MAKE it WORK!

Make a model of the Saturn V rocket (far right). Look at the models on the right to see the different stages of the Apollo 11 mission.

You will need

glue	balsa wood
tape	a craft knife
wire	thin cardboard
a saw	cardboard tube
paint	Earth and moon from page 15
stickers	a thick and thin wooden dowel
scissors	

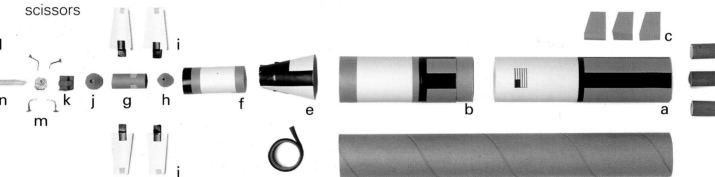

1 Cut a 7-in.- and 9-in.- length of cardboard tube, **a** and **b**. Decorate as shown. Leave $^3/_8$ in. of **b** uncovered; cut a slit in it and fold the edges so that they overlap. Insert **b** into **a**.

2 Cut three cardboard stabilizer fins, **c**, glue in position, as shown far right. Cut and paint three short, thin dowels, **d**. Glue them to **a**.

3 Make a 3-in.-long cone, **e**. Cut a 3-in. piece of thick dowel, **f**. Decorate as shown.

4 Cut a short, thin dowel, **g**. Make two cones, **h** and **j**; glue to **g**, as shown in 10, right.

5 Cut out four protective covers from thin cardboard, **i**. Tape the covers to the top of **f** (see 3 above).

6 For the lunar module, cut two balsa-wood shapes, **k** and **l**. Glue them together as shown in 6, right. Attach four wires, **m**, to make legs. Place the module inside the protective cover, **f** and **i**.

7 For the launch escape tower, **n**, ask an adult to shape a piece of thin dowel at both ends, using a craft knife. Paint it and glue it to **j**.

Stages of the Apollo 11 mission

1. Shortly after takeoff, the first stage of the Saturn V rocket fell away. The second stage carried Apollo higher before it, too, fell away.

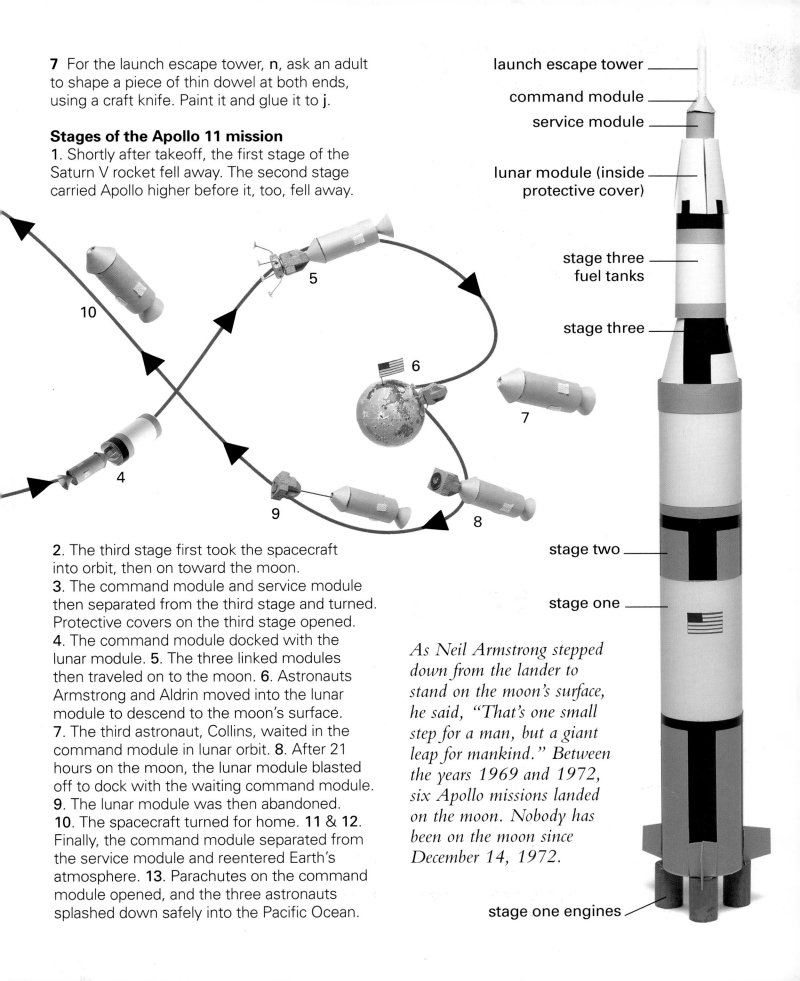

launch escape tower

command module

service module

lunar module (inside protective cover)

stage three fuel tanks

stage three

stage two

stage one

stage one engines

2. The third stage first took the spacecraft into orbit, then on toward the moon.
3. The command module and service module then separated from the third stage and turned. Protective covers on the third stage opened.
4. The command module docked with the lunar module. **5**. The three linked modules then traveled on to the moon. **6**. Astronauts Armstrong and Aldrin moved into the lunar module to descend to the moon's surface.
7. The third astronaut, Collins, waited in the command module in lunar orbit. **8**. After 21 hours on the moon, the lunar module blasted off to dock with the waiting command module.
9. The lunar module was then abandoned.
10. The spacecraft turned for home. **11 & 12**. Finally, the command module separated from the service module and reentered Earth's atmosphere. **13**. Parachutes on the command module opened, and the three astronauts splashed down safely into the Pacific Ocean.

As Neil Armstrong stepped down from the lander to stand on the moon's surface, he said, "That's one small step for a man, but a giant leap for mankind." Between the years 1969 and 1972, six Apollo missions landed on the moon. Nobody has been on the moon since December 14, 1972.

Eclipses are the biggest shadows you will ever see. A solar eclipse occurs when the moon passes between the sun and Earth, casting its shadow on Earth. In a lunar eclipse, Earth's shadow covers the moon. The moon's shadow is smaller than Earth, so a solar eclipse can be seen only where the shadow falls. But a lunar eclipse can be seen from anywhere on Earth that is facing the moon.

MAKE it WORK!
Use the model you made on page 6 to see how eclipses of the sun and moon happen.

This is how the sun, Earth, and moon line up in a lunar eclipse, which can happen twice a year.

Although the sun is 400 times bigger than the moon, it is also 400 times farther away. This is why they appear to be almost the same size.

This is how the sun, moon, and Earth are lined up during a solar eclipse. The moon blocks out the sun's light almost completely.

Earth lies between the sun and the moon, casting a dark shadow on the moon.

People on the night side of Earth see the moon vanish into shadow for an hour or more.

As the moon moves in its orbit, it comes between Earth and the sun. The moon casts a shadow over Earth's surface.

The eclipse is only total at the center of the shadow. The longest time a total eclipse can last is just under eight minutes.

The first person to look at the stars and planets with a telescope was probably the great Italian scientist Galileo, nearly 400 years ago. Using a simple telescope, much like the one shown on this page, he drew sketches of the mountains on the moon. He also discovered that Jupiter has moons and that the **Milky Way** is a countless mass of stars.

You will need
two magnifying lenses
cardboard tubes
scissors
tape
cardboard

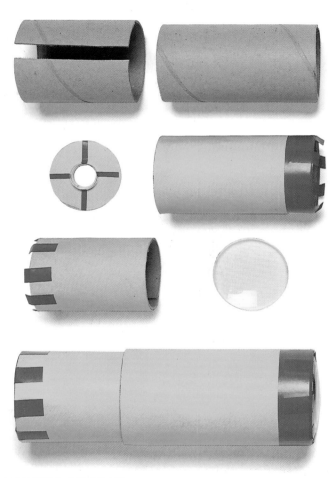

1 You will need to experiment to find out how long the telescope tube should be. Stand by a window and hold one lens at arm's length. Hold another lens to one eye. Slowly bring the first lens toward the second until you can see a clear image of the scene outside through both lenses (the image will be upside down). Try different pairs of lenses to find the best combination.

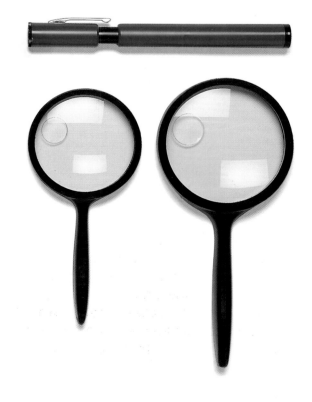

MAKE it WORK!
Construct a simple astronomical telescope with two magnifying lenses. Lenses are curved disks of glass. The lens through which the light enters the telescope is the **objective** lens. The second lens is the **eyepiece**.

2 Cut a piece of tube about an inch longer than the distance needed between the lenses. Cut this tube in half. Make a slit along the length of one of the tubes and overlap the edges slightly, so that it slides inside the other tube.

3 Fix the lenses to either end of the telescope tube using tape, as shown. Cut out a circle of cardboard for the eyepiece, shown left, and tape in place.

To study the moon through your telescope, slide the tubes in and out to **focus** the image sharply.

BE CAREFUL! Never look at the sun through a telescope or binoculars or with your naked eye. You could be blinded.

Using your solarscope you can study sunspots. These are cooler areas on the sun's surface. They move slowly from east to west because the sun is spinning.

A safe way to study the sun is to use a solarscope. Cut a hole in a large sheet of cardboard so that it just fits over one lens of a pair of binoculars. Put the binoculars on a pole and point them at the sun. **Do not look through the binoculars!** Cast an image of the sun on a piece of white cardboard behind the eyepiece.

Modern astronomers use telescopes with huge mirrors instead of objective lenses. These are often used in observatories on remote mountaintop sites where the air is clear. Space telescopes view the planets from above Earth's atmosphere. The Hubble Space Telescope was launched in 1990 and has a main mirror 8 ft. across.

22 Orbits and Gravity

Orbits are the circular or **elliptical** courses that planets and satellites follow, repeating their motion over and over again. There is always a massive object at the center of a planet's or moon's orbit. The sun is at the center of Earth's orbit, and Earth is at the center of the moon's orbit. It is the force of **gravity** between the objects that keeps the orbit going—like the pull on a weighted string when you whirl it in a circle.

MAKE it WORK!

Try drawing orbits. Some orbits are circles. Others are stretched circles called ellipses.

To draw an ellipse you will need

pencils   paper
thumbtacks   string
corkboard

1 Pin a sheet of paper to the corkboard.

2 Tie a loop of string and fix it to the board with two thumbtacks about 3 in. apart.

3 Stretch the loop with a pencil. Draw an ellipse by moving the pencil around the pins, keeping the string taut.

Experiment with the spacing of the pins and the length of the loop to draw different shaped ellipses. The two pins are at points called the **foci** of the ellipse. In our solar system, the sun sits at one focus of each planet's elliptical orbit.

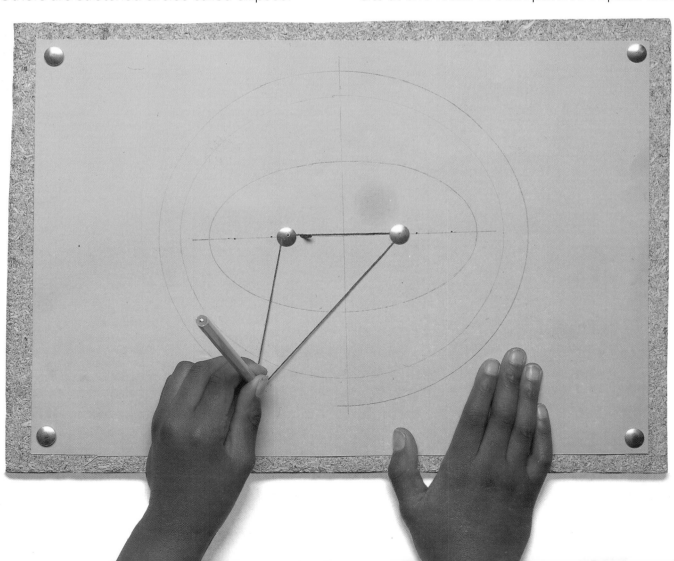

Studying orbits

The planets farthest from the sun travel more slowly in their orbits than those that are nearby. This model shows how an orbit speeds up as it gets smaller.

1 Ask an adult to help you drill a hole in the block just big enough for the dowel. Fix the dowel firmly in place.

2 Tie one end of the string to the top of the pole. Tape the other end to the ball. Launch the ball into orbit around the pole.

What happens to the ball's speed as the string winds around the pole and the orbit gets smaller?

Into orbit

A satellite must be launched at the right speed and angle if it is to stay in orbit around Earth. If it goes too fast, it will escape from Earth's gravity and disappear into space. Too slow, and it will spiral back into the atmosphere and burn up.

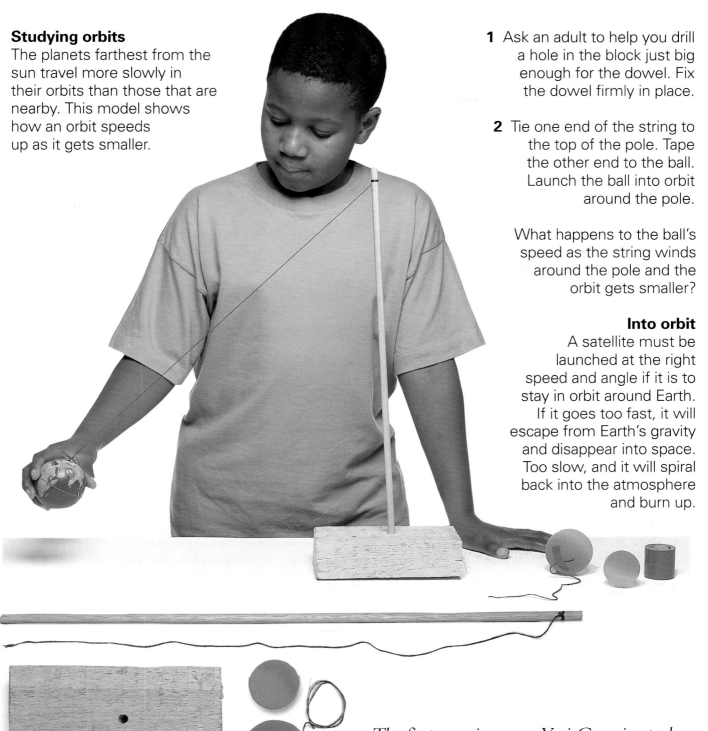

You will need
a rubber ball
a wooden block
a wooden dowel
tape
string
a hand drill

The first man in space, Yuri Gagarin, took just 80 minutes to orbit Earth in 1961. This is the orbital time, or period, for any satellite just above Earth's atmosphere. Television satellites take 24 hours to orbit Earth. These satellites keep step with Earth's rotation so that they are always over the same place on Earth.

The sun is at the center of our solar system. Orbiting the sun are nine planets, their moons, and millions of smaller objects such as asteroids and comets. From the sun out, the planets are Mercury, Venus, Earth, Mars, Jupiter, Saturn, Uranus, Neptune, and Pluto. Each planet moves at a different speed in its orbit. The inner planets travel much faster than the more distant planets.

MAKE it WORK!

Move the planets around this model solar system calendar to compare how long it takes them to orbit the sun.

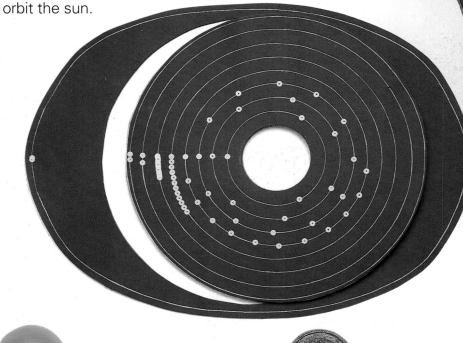

The stickers on each orbit, up to and including Saturn, represent one month. After Saturn, they represent one year.

You will need

adhesive paper rings	cardboard
10 rubber or plastic balls	scissors
a drawing compass, wire	glue, paint
a flashlight	an awl
a large sheet of blue poster board	

1 Paint the balls to make the nine planets, as shown above. Ask an adult to help you make holes through the balls using an awl and fix them onto the wires. The sun is made with half a plastic ball, fixed over a flashlight.

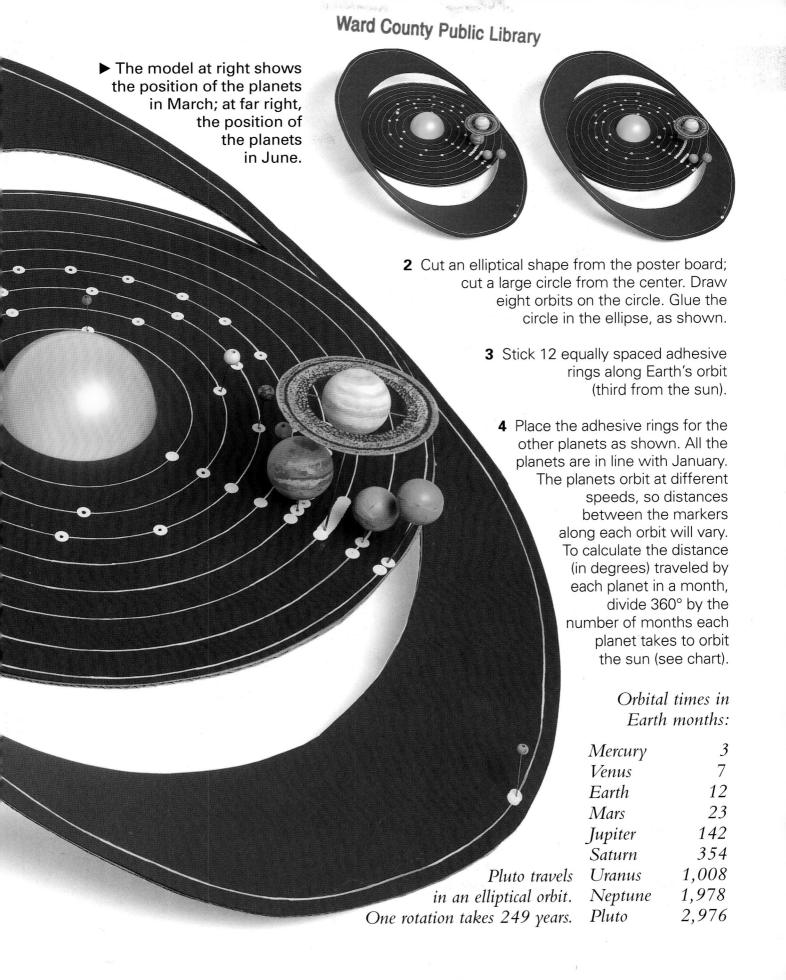

► The model at right shows the position of the planets in March; at far right, the position of the planets in June.

2 Cut an elliptical shape from the poster board; cut a large circle from the center. Draw eight orbits on the circle. Glue the circle in the ellipse, as shown.

3 Stick 12 equally spaced adhesive rings along Earth's orbit (third from the sun).

4 Place the adhesive rings for the other planets as shown. All the planets are in line with January. The planets orbit at different speeds, so distances between the markers along each orbit will vary. To calculate the distance (in degrees) traveled by each planet in a month, divide 360° by the number of months each planet takes to orbit the sun (see chart).

Orbital times in Earth months:

Mercury	*3*
Venus	*7*
Earth	*12*
Mars	*23*
Jupiter	*142*
Saturn	*354*
Uranus	*1,008*
Neptune	*1,978*
Pluto	*2,976*

Pluto travels in an elliptical orbit. One rotation takes 249 years.

What's inside a planet? If you sliced Earth in half, you would find it has a hot, metal core of mainly nickel and iron. Surrounding this core are layers of rock and other metals. We live on Earth's outer crust, a thin layer of rock that is between 4 and 24 miles thick.

3 With an adult's help, use a craft knife to cut slits (as shown below right) in each pair of planet disks. Cut a large section in each (as shown below far right). Slide the disks together to assemble your planets. Fold the large section upward as shown. Then mount your planets on wires, securing them with tape.

What are the planets like?
Venus is almost the same size as Earth and probably has a similar core surrounded by layers of

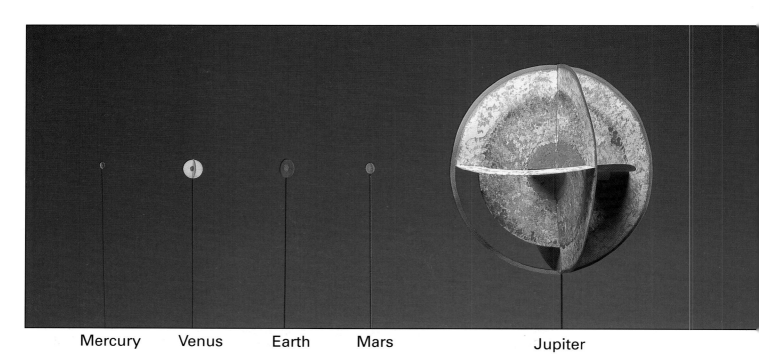

| Mercury | Venus | Earth | Mars | Jupiter |

MAKE it WORK!
These models show what scientists think the planets look like on the inside.

You will need
tape	scissors
paint	a craft knife
wire and cardboard	a drawing compass

1 Each planet is made from two identical cardboard disks. Use the compass to draw circles to the scale of the planets (see table far right).

2 Draw rings to show the different layers within each planet and paint them different colors.

rock. Venus has a dense atmosphere, but this is nothing like Earth's. It is filled with acid droplets and is as hot as the surface of Mercury.

Earth is the watery planet. Water covers more than two-thirds of Earth's surface. The average surface temperature of 80 °F (27 °C) is just right for life, and it is the only planet on which life is known.

Mars, the red planet, is about half the diameter of Earth. It has a small iron core surrounded by rocky layers. It has a very thin atmosphere and is much colder than Earth.

Jupiter is the largest planet. Unlike the four inner planets (Mercury, Venus, Earth, and Mars), it is not solid. It has a solid rock core, surrounded by a very dense atmosphere of cold, swirling gas. A spacecraft could not land on Jupiter—it would sink into the gas.

Jupiter has a huge, swirling weather system the size of the planet Earth on its surface, called the Great Red Spot. Scientists are still not sure how Jupiter was formed.

Saturn, Neptune, and Uranus are all "gas giants" like Jupiter. Saturn has spectacular rings made from millions of tiny rocks orbiting like moons. Jupiter, Uranus, and Neptune also have rings. Draw the rings on a cardboard disk and attach them with wires to your models.

Pluto is the smallest of all the planets and the most distant from the sun. It is believed to be made up of a rocky core surrounded by layers of ice and frozen gas.

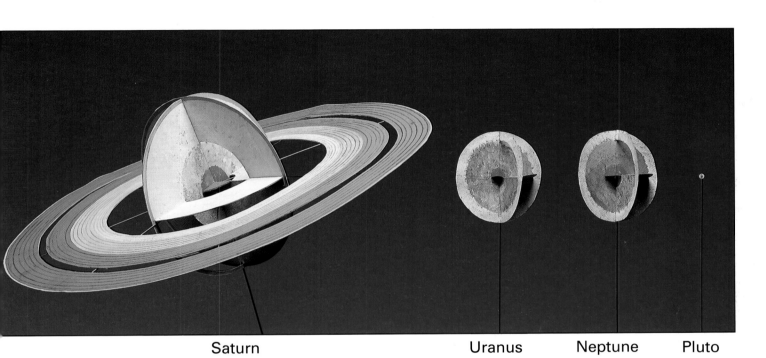

Saturn · Uranus · Neptune · Pluto

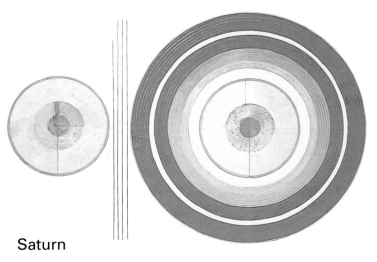

Saturn

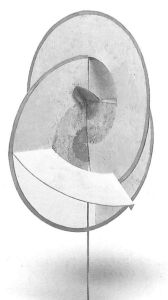

Sizes of planets in relation to Earth's diameter:

Mercury	*0.4*
Venus	*0.9*
Earth	*1*
Mars	*0.5*
Jupiter	*11*
Saturn	*9*
Uranus	*4*
Neptune	*4*
Pluto	*0.2*

28 Meteoroids and Comets

Meteoroids are pieces of rock often left behind by **comets**. As meteoroids enter Earth's atmosphere, friction makes them burn up and they become shooting stars. The moon has no atmosphere to protect it from collisions. It is covered with craters made by meteorites hitting its surface.

You will need
newspapers
flour or damp sand
a large tray or oven dish
ball bearings or marbles

1 Protect your work surface with newspaper. Fill the tray with flour or damp sand. Drop the meteors into the tray to make model craters.

Experiment to see how the size of the meteor and the height from which you drop it affects the crater.

A meteoroid that enters the atmosphere is called a **meteor**. If it lands without burning up, it is called a meteorite.

MAKE it WORK!
The surface of the moon is pitted with craters. Make your own moon surface and see how craters are formed. There are meteorite craters on Earth, too. The Barringer meteorite landed in Arizona, leaving a crater almost a mile wide.

Comets are balls of rock, ice, and frozen gas that orbit the sun in elliptical paths. As comets get close to the sun, some of the gas boils off, making the comet look as if it has a tail, and pieces of rock come away. These rock fragments become meteoroids. Halley's Comet comes close to Earth every 76 years. Last seen in 1986, it is due to reappear in 2062.

Asteroids are potato-shaped lumps of rock left over from the time when the planets formed. Most asteroids travel in a belt between the orbits of Mars and Jupiter. With some cardboard and paint, you can add the asteroid belts to your solar system model.

The **Trojans** are two groups of asteroids that follow the same orbit as Jupiter around the sun. Make and paint two cardboard asteroid groups like those shown below for the Trojans. Place them in Jupiter's orbit on your model.

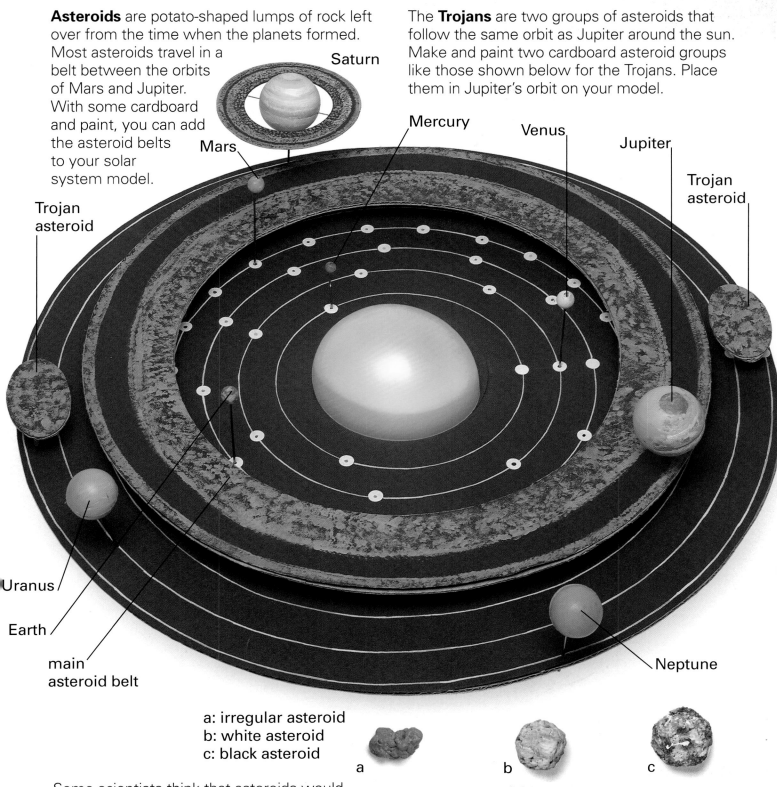

Saturn

Mercury

Venus

Jupiter

Trojan asteroid

Mars

Trojan asteroid

Uranus

Earth

main asteroid belt

Neptune

a: irregular asteroid
b: white asteroid
c: black asteroid

a
b
c

Some scientists think that asteroids would make good "stepping stones" for the **colonization** of space (see p 30-31). Space stations could be set up on larger asteroids. They could also be mined for raw materials.

There are millions of asteroids orbiting the asteroid belts. They range in size from grains of sand to lumps bigger than Mt. Everest. The biggest, called Ceres, is 567 mi in diameter.

Imagine climbing aboard a spacecraft and setting out to explore the solar system, perhaps stopping to visit a colony on Mars and going on to see the asteroids. There are plans for a trip to Mars within your lifetime. So far, the farthest space journey made by humans has been to the moon. However, robot probes have landed on, or flown by, every planet except Pluto.

You will need

tape and glue	wire
a ping-pong ball	beads
a battery and wires	scissors
a bulb and bulb holder	poster board
polystyrene packing foam	a craft knife
fishing wire or wooden dowel	a plastic ball
a transparent colored plastic tube	

1 Use a plastic ball cut in half for the probe's body, **e**. Make a hole big enough for the bulb to go through and two holes for the bulb wires. To make the beacon, **f**, follow steps **a** to **d** below. Tape the battery to the probe's body.

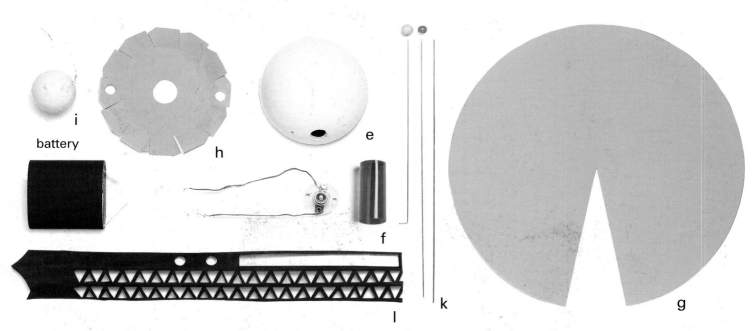

battery

i

h

e

f

k

l

g

2 To make the probe dish, **g**, cut out a circle of poster board 12 in. in diameter. Cut a segment out of it, as above. Overlap the cut edges and tape or glue them together. The dish points to Earth to transmit and receive radio signals.

MAKE it WORK!

Make your own space probe based on the Voyager probes. These probes are known as fly-by probes, because their **sensors** record information as they pass close to the planets.

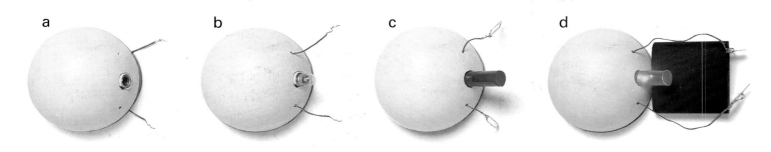

a   b   c   d

3 Make the probe platform, **h**, by cutting out a circle with a 6-in. diameter. Make 12 cuts, $^3/_8$ in. deep, around the circle, then bend and glue into shape. Glue the platform to the probe body, as shown below.

4 For the atmosphere probe, **i**, glue half a ping-pong ball to the back of the platform. For the camera, stick a tube of black poster board onto a wire and tape it to the body. For the antennas, **k**, glue beads to straight wires and attach as shown.

6 Make asteroids with painted pieces of polystyrene foam stuck onto lengths of wire.

7 Tape your fly-by probe to a wooden dowel glued to a base board.

The Voyager 2 probe was launched in 1977. Since then it has transmitted thousands of pictures back to Earth, enabling scientists to make many new discoveries.

5 For the boom, **l**, ask an adult to help you cut and fold a piece of black poster board into a boom shape as shown left. The boom here folds into a triangular shape. Yours can be simpler. Glue the boom to the dish.

Two Viking probes landed on Mars in 1976. They sent back 3,000 photographic images, took soil samples that were examined in a specially built laboratory, and measured the temperature and wind speed on the surface. No recognizable signs of life were found.

The space pioneers who eventually set off to colonize Mars and the asteroids will have to create their own sealed environment in which to live. Growing plants for food and providing enough oxygen will be their main priority. The pioneers will use solar energy and will have to recycle all their water and waste materials.

During the day, the plants' green leaves collect energy from sunlight, which they use to convert water from the soil and carbon dioxide from the air into a simple sugar called glucose. This process is called **photosynthesis**. As the leaves make glucose, they also make oxygen. Plants and the tiny animals (worms or insects) in the bottle use the food (glucose) and oxygen to grow. When they do this they release water and carbon dioxide. This is called respiration.

In a bottle garden, the sun's energy constantly recycles oxygen, water, and carbon dioxide between the soil, the living things, and the air. A space colony could work in a similar way.

You will need
water
a trowel
potting soil
a large glass jar with a lid
four plants (small, well-established plants that like a warm, damp atmosphere, such as ferns, miniature ivy, African violets, mosses, begonias, and small spider plants, are the best)

MAKE it WORK!
A space colony could work in a similar way to a bottle garden. Plants sealed inside the bottle need only the energy of sunlight to grow.

1 Fill the bottom of the jar with a layer of potting soil, about 4- to 6-in. deep. Level it off and then pat the soil firm.

2 Gently remove your plants from their pots. Using the trowel, make holes in the soil large enough to accommodate the roots of the plants. Put the plants in the holes and replace the soil, pressing it down firmly.

3 Water the garden carefully. The potting soil should be moist but not too wet.

Biosphere 2 is an experimental environment in Arizona that is run like a space colony. Six people lived inside a glass and steel dome for two years to see if it was possible to grow all their own food and recycle their water and air, sealed off from the outside world. They lost weight and had some problems with the atmosphere, but they survived. More experiments like this will be essential before real space colonies can be set up. The colonists won't be able to run to the supermarket if they run out of something!

4 If you want to make your garden look more like a space colony, place some model people, animals, and space vehicles among the plants.

5 Put the lid on the bottle and seal it tightly.

6 Put your garden where it will receive plenty of sunlight but not extreme, direct sunlight. The plants should grow without extra water. If the inside of the bottle steams up, take off the lid for an hour or so to let it clear.

The sun is a medium-sized star on the edge of the Milky Way. There are billions of other stars in our galaxy. The nearest star to Earth, apart from the sun, is called Proxima Centauri. Its light takes more than four years to reach Earth.

You will need

tape, glue	tissue paper and cotton
a strip of wood	seven bulbs and holders
poster board, scissors	a battery and wire
different sized rubber balls	a hole punch
cellophane candy wrappers	screws

1 Screw the bulb holders to the strip of wood and connect the wires, as shown below.

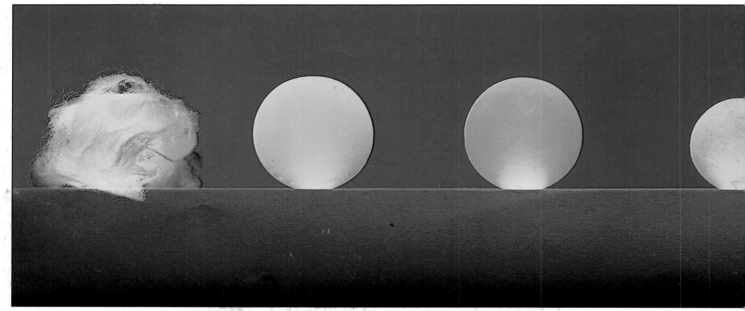

dense cloud of dust star is born young star star condenses

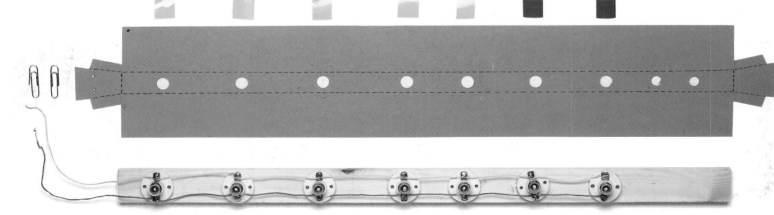

MAKE it WORK!

This model shows the different stages that a star goes through over millions of years, from its beginnings as a gas cloud to its death as a supernova or even a black hole.

2 Cut out the poster board and punch a hole for each bulb, as shown. Fold it into a cover that the lights will fit under.

3 Glue the cover to the wood. Then stick colored candy wrappers over the holes.

4 To show the birth of a star as a hot gas cloud, wrap a ball in cotton.

5 Place the balls on top of the lights. Follow the sequence below to show the stages of a star's life. Connect the wires to the battery.

glows steadily for millions of years. The sun has been burning for 5 billion years and is about halfway through its life. Finally, the energy of the star is used up. As it starts to cool down, it expands to become a red giant and eventually collapses. Heavy stars may vanish in a fantastic explosion, or supernova. A dense core called a neutron star, or white dwarf, is left behind. The heaviest stars then collapse again, creating a black hole.

steady star   red giant   nebula   white dwarf   black globe

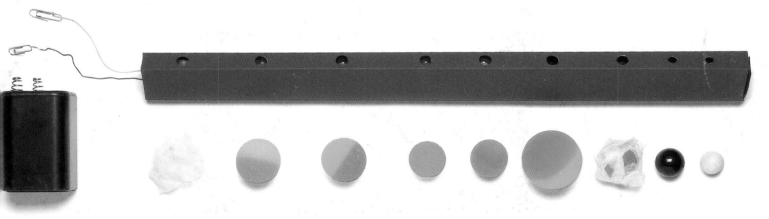

A star is born from clouds of gas in space. As the cloud condenses, it heats up. Eventually, nuclear reactions start, and the star shines.

At first a star glows dully. Then as it gets hotter, it turns orange, then yellow, then white hot. A star

In 1054, the Chinese recorded a star bright enough to be seen during the day. It was a supernova called the Crab Nebula. We can still see its remains today.

A planetarium is a motion picture of the sky. The patterns and movements of the stars are projected onto a dome above your head that represents the night sky. Stars appear to be fixed to a distant **celestial** sphere, but they are, in fact, at different distances from Earth and look bigger and brighter, or smaller and dimmer, according to how far they are from us. The planetarium's projector turns to show how the stars seem to move as Earth spins on its axis.

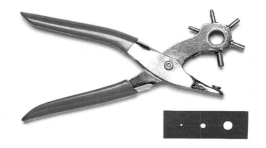

MAKE it WORK!

Making your own planetarium will help you to learn the names of the stars and their constellations and will make finding them in the night sky a lot easier.

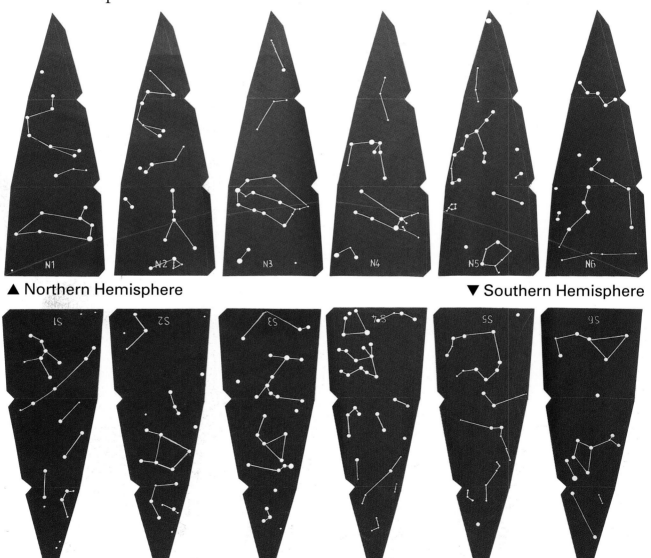

▲ Northern Hemisphere

▼ Southern Hemisphere

You will need

a hole punch   tracing paper   dark blue poster board
plain and luminous paints   a flashlight   glue

1 Cut 24 identical poster board segments, as
shown below, 13 in. x 5 in. at the base.

2 Using a star chart or globe (right), trace the
positions of the bright stars. Without turning
the paper over, transfer your marks to the
segments. Number the segments, so you
will know the order in which they fit together.

3 Make a hole for each star, using the punch. As
stars vary in brightness, or **magnitude**, punch
larger holes for the brighter stars. Mark the
constellations with luminous paint.

▲ Northern Hemisphere

▼ Southern Hemisphere

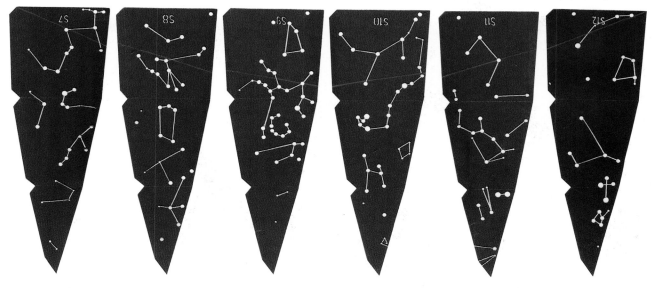

Complete your planetarium

Now you can complete the model planetarium that you started to make on page 37. Once all the stars have been punched with holes and joined to make constellations, you will need to glue all the segments together. Make sure that you glue them in the correct order to make the Northern and Southern hemispheres.

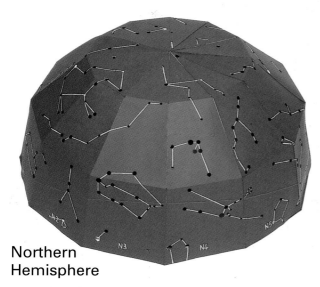

Northern Hemisphere

4 To make a star dome or a globe that you can view from the outside, lay the segments in order with the star patterns facing out.

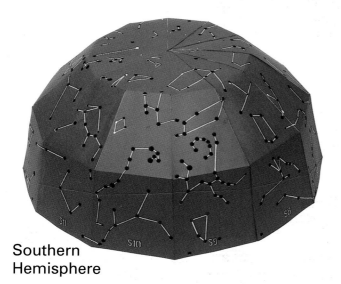

Southern Hemisphere

5 Now fold and glue the segments together to make north and south celestial hemispheres. Make sure the segments are in order.

6 To view the stars, stand the hemispheres over a flashlight or a low-wattage lamp and turn off the lights in the room. The stars will shine just as they do on a clear night.

Although the stars are constantly moving, they are so distant they appear fixed. Because of this, we can map them on a celestial sphere.

If you lived at the North Pole, you would be able to see all the stars in the northern celestial hemisphere when it is dark. At the South Pole you would have a clear view of all the southern stars.

People who live between the equator and the North Pole or the South Pole see different stars at different times of the year. This is because Earth is orbiting the sun, and the dark side of Earth faces a slightly different direction each night.

North of the equator, in the United States for example, you see all the northern stars and some of the southern ones during the year. South of the equator, in Australia or New Zealand for example, all of the southern stars and some of the northern ones are visible. However, if you live on the equator, during the course of a year it is possible to see the complete celestial sphere.

Polaris, the Pole Star, lies almost directly above the North Pole. If you find Polaris, you can work out which way you are facing and will never lose your direction on a starry night.

The red line on the model is called the plane of the ecliptic. This is the path that the sun seems to take through the stars during the year.

If you want to see the stars in your model in exactly the same way that you would view them in a planetarium, then you have to be able to look up into it. In this case, you will need to glue the segments together with the star patterns facing inward. If you do not put it together in this way, the patterns will look back to front.

If you watch the stars during the course of a night, they seem to move in the sky, turning around Polaris, the Pole Star, in the north. But really the stars are fixed, and it is Earth that is spinning. Try turning your model planetarium above your head; then keep the planetarium still and turn your head instead. Both actions make the stars appear to move.

Have you ever looked up at the clouds and thought you could see faces or animals? Stars also make shapes in the sky. In our mind's eye we can draw lines between the stars to join them and make patterns called constellations. The ancient Greeks created legends about the figures they saw in the stars. They gave the constellations names, such as Orion the hunter, Taurus the bull, and Aquarius the water gatherer.

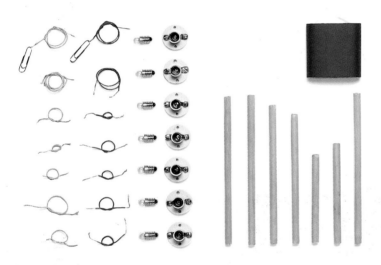

MAKE it WORK!

This model shows how stars in the Big Dipper (which is part of the Ursa Major, or Great Bear, constellation) are arranged in three dimensions. The stars make the pattern we see only when they are viewed from one particular direction.

You will need

wires
a glue gun
a hand drill
yellow paint
a wooden dowel
dark blue poster board
a base board (8 in. x 12 in.)
seven bulbs and seven holders

scissors
a battery
insulated wire

1 Cut out a piece of poster board that will overlap your base board by 2 in. Cover base board with the cardboard, sticking it down with glue. Mark out and rule the cardboard with a ³/₄-in. square grid, as shown below. The squares represent light-years (the distance traveled by light in a year).

2 Using the grid as your guide, ask an adult to help you drill seven holes big enough for the dowel posts, as shown below.

3 Cut the dowel into seven lengths, as shown left, and glue them into the holes.

4 Glue the bulb holders onto the top of the dowels and screw in the bulbs.

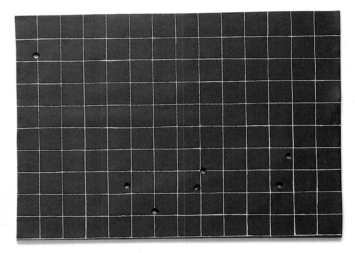

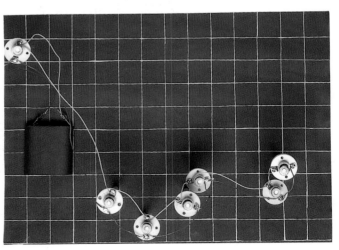

5 Wire the bulbs as shown above and connect the battery.

Alkaid   Mizar Alioth   Megrez Phekda   Merak   Dubhe

It's best to view your constellation from a distance in a dark room, or outside on a dark night.

The Big Dipper, or Plow, is part of the Ursa Major constellation. It is one of the easiest star patterns to find in the northern sky. The stars on the right, Merak and Dubhe, point up to Polaris.

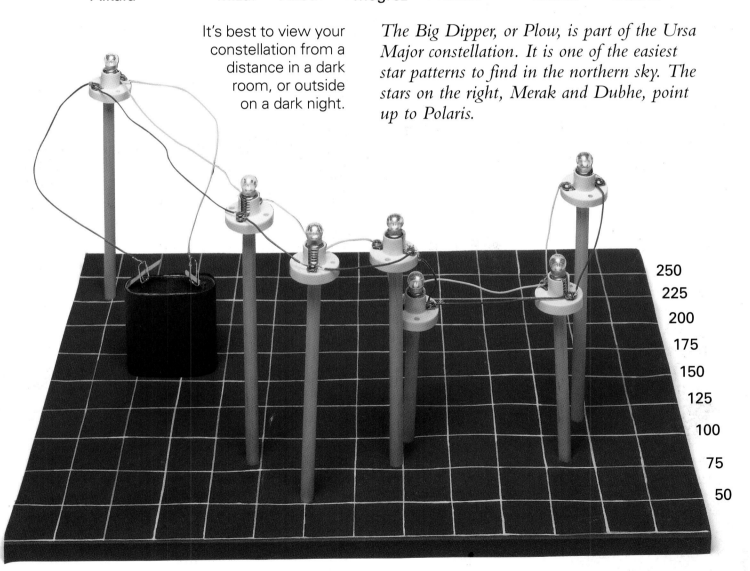

250
225
200
175
150
125
100
75
50

Walk around the model to see how the shape of the Plow changes from different viewpoints.

Astronomers use 88 named constellations to find their way around the night sky.

As Earth spins, the stars seem to move in the sky. Earth's night side faces in different directions at different times of the year, so some stars that can be seen in winter are not visible in summer.

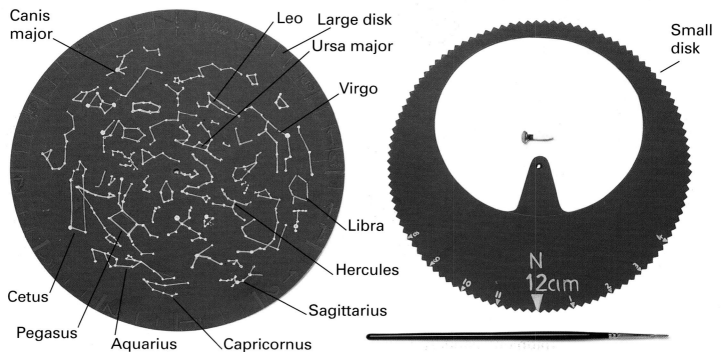

Canis major — Leo — Large disk — Ursa major — Virgo — Libra — Hercules — Sagittarius — Capricornus — Aquarius — Pegasus — Cetus — Small disk — N 12cm

Finding constellations in the night sky can be difficult. A planisphere is a special chart that shows where constellations are at different times of the year.

MAKE it WORK!

You can make a model star planisphere. If you want an accurate planisphere, you must buy one specially made for the **latitude** where you live. The star finder shown on this page works for northern Europe and the northern parts of North America.

You will need
cardboard
scissors
luminous paints
a magnetic compass

glue
a star chart
a brad
a paintbrush

1 Cut out two circles from cardboard: one should be about an inch smaller in diameter than the other.

2 Buy or borrow a star chart. Make a photo copy of the stars that are visible from the Northern Hemisphere. Glue the copy onto your larger disk. Trace over the constellations with luminous paint.

3 Make 12 equally spaced marks around the large disk to represent the months. Using your paints, number the months from 1 to 12 and then divide each into four and mark each quarter, as shown above left.

4 Cut a window from the small disk, as shown above. Leave a "finger" of cardboard reaching to the center.

5 Mark the hours, from 8 P.M. to 4 A.M., on the edge of the small disk. The space between each hour should be half the space given to each month on the big disk. Mark north with an N and an arrow, at 12 midnight, as above.

6 Make a hole in the center of both disks and join them together with the brad.

To use the star finder, turn the upper disk to line up the time with the month. Now, use a compass to find magnetic North and turn to face it, holding your star finder in front of you. If the night sky is clear, you should be able to see the stars shown in the window.

▲ The night sky at midnight, January 1

Try to view the night sky in an area where there are no street lights; otherwise you will only be able to see the brightest stars.

If you buy a planisphere for a different latitude, the window will be in a different position on the upper disk.

With your naked eye you can see about 3,000 stars, but with a pair of binoculars you can see many more. All the individual stars we can see are part of a huge "star city," or galaxy, called the Milky Way. There may be as many as 100 billion stars in the Milky Way, but it is not the only galaxy in the universe. There are billions of galaxies, each made from gas, dust, and billions of stars.

Galaxies are made up of billions of stars, many of which are like our sun. Most are so far away that they can only be seen with the use of a powerful telescope. The light from the farthest galaxies takes millions of years to reach Earth. Our galaxy is the Milky Way, which is thought to contain around 100 billion stars. It has spiral arms like the model below. Our sun lives in one of the arms.

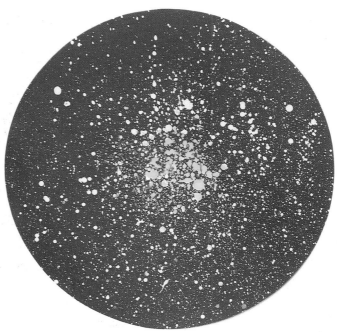

▲ A galaxy

People still watch the sky, and astronomy is one of the few sciences in which amateurs can make valuable contributions. Astronomical societies provide information on astronomy for their members by publishing newsletters and holding meetings. Write to an astronomical society; find out what other astronomers are looking for. What discoveries might you make?

Throughout history, people have asked many questions about the universe. One of the great puzzles was "Does the universe have an edge, or does it go on forever?" The great scientist Albert Einstein thought that space need not have an edge because it may be curved.

MAKE it WORK!
The models here will help you understand two key ideas about the universe: the way a massive star curves the space around it, and how expansion makes galaxies move apart.

When a star dies, gravity makes it collapse. If the star was a giant, it could form a black hole.

2 Cut a strip of cardboard, 1 yd. long x 3 in. wide. Curl it into a ring and tape the ends, as shown below. Stretch the rubber over the ring and secure it with tape.

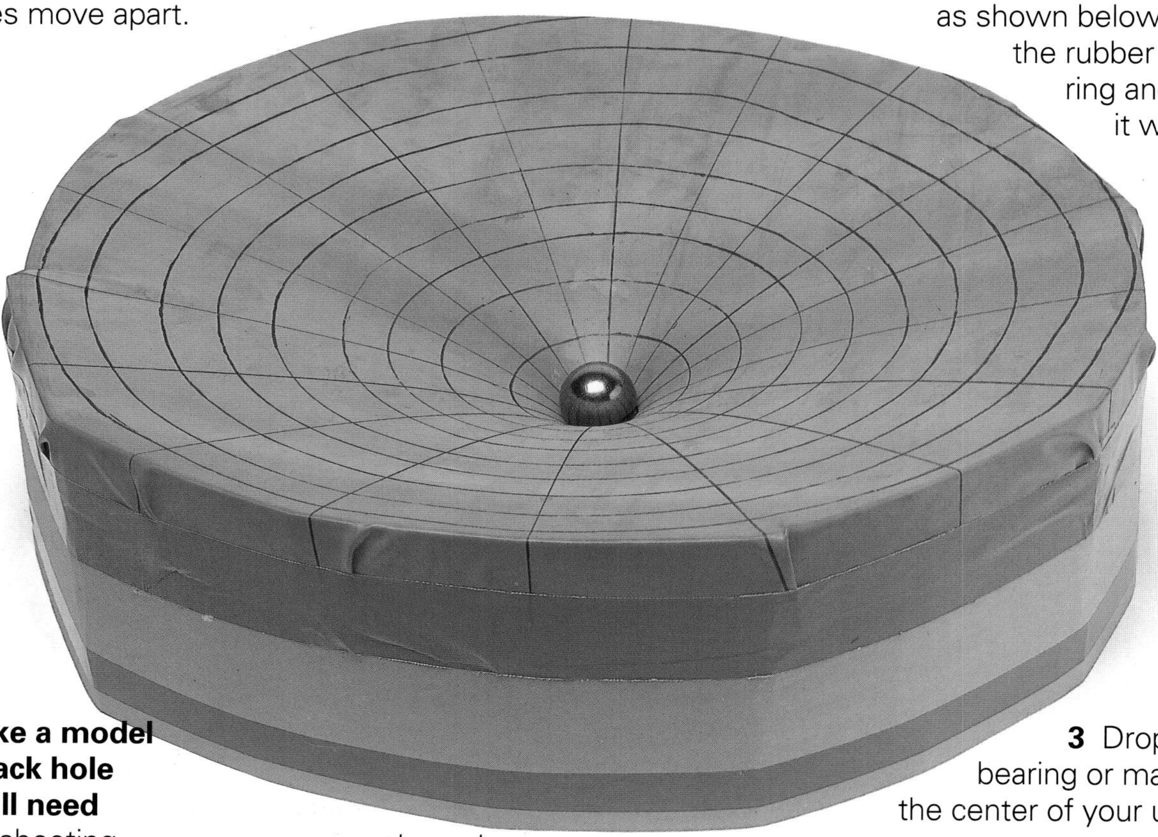

To make a model of a black hole you will need

rubber sheeting	strong tape
heavy cardboard	a felt-tip pen
a drawing compass	a protractor
a heavy ball bearing or marble	scissors

1 Cut a 36-in.-diameter circle of rubber. Draw circles on it 2 in. apart. Use a protractor to measure diagonal lines across every 20°.

3 Drop the ball bearing or marble into the center of your universe.

When the rubber sheet is flat, the lines on the grid are evenly spaced. This shows what normal space is like. When you add the ball bearing, the grid stretches—you can see how the universe curves around a massive star. A curved universe need not have an edge, just as the surface of a football has no edge.

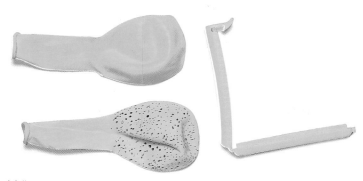

Every galaxy on the balloon moves away from every other galaxy. This is exactly what happens in space as the universe expands. The galaxies remain the same size but get farther apart from one another.

On your model universe, notice how more distant galaxies move farther apart, each time you blow air into the balloon, than galaxies that are neighbors. This is just what astronomers see when they look into space through powerful telescopes. The farther a galaxy is from the Milky Way (our galaxy), the faster it is moving away.

When astronomers look at distant galaxies, they can see them moving away from us. This shows that the universe is getting bigger all the time. Most scientists believe that the universe was formed by a huge explosion, called the big bang, 15 billion years ago. Ever since then, space has continued to expand.

To make an expanding universe you will need
a ruler
balloons
felt-tip pens

1 Using a felt-tip pen, draw galaxies all over a flat balloon, as shown at the top of the page.

2 Blow up the balloon, a little at a time. As you blow it up, the distance between galaxies grows larger. Measure some of these distances.

Astronomers think that the expansion of the universe is slowing down. Perhaps one day it will stop completely and will start to collapse again. This would be similar to a balloon shrinking when you let air out of it. If this does happen, everything in the universe will collapse, and it will end with what scientists call the "big crunch!" But don't worry, the "big crunch" is not expected to happen for billions of years.

Asteroid Asteroids are rocks that range in size from a diameter of one mile to a few hundred miles. Most of them orbit the sun in the asteroid belt that lies between the orbits of Jupiter and Mars.

Axis An axis is an imaginary line around which something turns. Earth spins around an axis running between the North and South poles.

Black holes These are holes in space where gravity is so strong that nothing, not even light, can escape once it has fallen in. They form when massive stars burn out and gravity crushes together the matter left over.

Calibrate This term refers to making or checking marks on a measuring scale, such as a ruler or a sundial.

Celestial This means anything to do with the sky. When we look at the stars in the sky, we imagine that the stars are fixed to a revolving celestial sphere.

Colonize When a group of people move to a new place and settle there, this is called colonizing.

Comet A ball of rock, ice, and frozen gas that orbits the sun. When a comet comes near the sun, parts melt and boil off to form the comet's tail.

Compass (magnetic) This is an instrument with a magnetized needle that always points to the North Pole. It is used for finding direction.

Compass (drawing) This instrument is used to draw circles. It has two hinged legs: one leg acts as a fixed point, the other holds a pencil or a pen.

Eclipse An eclipse happens when the sun's light is blocked by Earth or the moon. A lunar eclipse occurs when Earth blocks the light between the sun and the moon.

Ellipse An ellipse is a special curved shape, which looks like a flattened or stretched circle. The orbits that some of the planets make around the sun are elliptical.

Energy When something has energy it can make things move, change, or warm up.

Equator The equator is an imaginary line around Earth halfway between the poles that divide the Northern and Southern hemispheres.

Eyepiece The eyepiece of a telescope is the lens through which we look.

Foci (plural of focus) An ellipse has two foci. These are two special points, like the center of a circle around which the ellipse is drawn. The sun sits at one focus of Earth's elliptical orbit.

Focus To focus means to concentrate light to make a clear picture. Telescopes collect and focus the light from planets and stars. The focus of a lens is the point at which the light from a distant object, such as a star, is concentrated when it passes through the lens.

Galaxy A group of billions of stars in space.

Gnomon The pointer that casts a shadow on a sundial.

Gravity The force that makes things feel heavy and pulls them toward the ground. The force of gravity keeps the moon orbiting Earth and the planets orbiting the sun.

Hemisphere Half of a sphere, like a dome. Earth is divided into two hemispheres—Northern and Southern.

Latitude The distance measured widthwise from the equator. The equator is 0°, while the North and South poles are at 90° latitude.

Lens A curved piece of glass or plastic, specially shaped to focus light.

Lunar Lunar refers to the moon; for example, the lunar surface.

Magnitude Another word for the brightness of a star, as seen from Earth.

Meteor The name given to a small piece of rock from space (a meteoroid) that has burned up on entering Earth's atmosphere.

Meteoroid A piece of rock or debris in space, often broken off from a comet.

Milky Way The Milky Way is our galaxy. The sun is just one of a billion stars that make up the Milky Way.

Nuclear reaction A change that happens when tiny particles from the center of atoms knock into each other. Nuclear reactions in stars give out the great amounts of energy that make stars shine.

Objective The objective lens of a telescope is the large lens that collects and focuses light from the stars.

Orbit The curved path followed by a planet, a moon, or a satellite as it spins around a more massive body.

Photosynthesis The process by which the green leaves on plants trap the energy of sunlight and use it to make food.

Sensors These are the thermometers, cameras, and other measuring instruments used on probes and satellites. They record information about a planet.

Solar Solar refers to the sun. For instance, in a solar eclipse, it is the sun's light that is blocked by the moon.

Solar panel A special panel that absorbs the sun's energy and converts it into electricity.

Space probes There are two types: fly-by probes and landers. A fly-by probe is a spacecraft sent to fly close to planets. Its purpose is to gather information, collect samples, and record pictures to beam back to Earth. A lander has the same function as a fly-by, but it lands on a planet's surface.

Trojans Two groups of asteroids that follow the same orbit as Jupiter around the sun. They travel in front of and behind Jupiter.